Expanding ESL, Civics, and Citizenship Education in Your Community

A Start-Up Guide

U.S. Citizenship and Immigration Services

U.S. Government Official Edition Notice

AUTHENTICATED
U.S. GOVERNMENT
INFORMATION
GPO

Use of ISBN

This is the Official U.S. Government edition of this publication and is herein identified to certify its authenticity. Use of the ISBN 978-0-16-084388-4 is for U.S. Government Printing Office Official Editions only. The Superintendent of Documents of the U.S. Government Printing Office requests that any reprinted edition clearly be labeled as a copy of the authentic work with a new ISBN.

The information presented in Expanding ESL, Civics, and Citizenship Education in Your Community: A Start-Up Guide is considered public information and may be distributed or copied without alteration unless otherwise specified. The citation should be:

U.S. Department of Homeland Security, U.S. Citizenship and Immigration Services, Office of Citizenship, Expanding ESL, Civics, and Citizenship Education in Your Community: A Start-Up Guide, Washington, DC, 2009.

U.S. Citizenship and Immigration Services (USCIS) has purchased the right to use many of the images in Expanding ESL, Civics, and Citizenship Education in Your Community: A Start-Up Guide. USCIS is licensed to use these images on a non-exclusive and non-transferable basis. All other rights to the images, including without limitation and copyright, are retained by the owner of the images. These images are not in the public domain and may not be used except as they appear as part of this publication.

For sale by the Superintendent of Documents, U.S. Government Printing Office
Internet: bookstore.gpo.gov   Phone: toll free (866) 512-1800;   DC area (202) 512-1800
Fax: (202) 512-2104 Mail: Stop IDCC, Washington, DC 20402-0001

ISBN 978-0-16-084388-4

Table of Contents

Gathering Information and Basic Resources ... 2
Determining Community Needs ... 2
Gathering Information ... 2
Meeting the Need ... 2

Program Design and Structure ... 3
Setting the Course for Your Program ... 3
Assessing Your Resources ... 3
Selecting the Target Audience ... 3
Finding a Site ... 3
Establishing a Program Framework and Mission ... 4
Program Structure and Instruction ... 5
Class Size ... 5
Instructional Approach ... 5
Enrollment Options ... 6

Staffing and Resources ... 6
Finding and Supporting Your Volunteers ... 6
Volunteer Positions ... 6
Volunteer Job Descriptions ... 7
Volunteer Tutor Recruitment ... 7
Introducing the Program to Volunteers ... 9
Volunteer Screening and Selection ... 9
Volunteer Orientation ... 10
Volunteer Support and Tutor Training ... 10
Local Resources ... 10
National Resources ... 10

Marketing Your Program to Students ... 12
Getting Students Involved ... 12
Student Recruitment ... 12
Student Registration and Orientation ... 13

Program Content and Instruction 14
Determining Student Educational Needs:
What and How to Teach 14
- Needs Assessment 14
- Topics Often Included in ESL/Civics Instruction 16
- Teaching Resources 16
- Teaching Techniques 17

Program Development 20
How to Strengthen Your Program 20
- Start-Up Costs and Sustainability 20
- Funding and Coordination 21
- Evaluating Program Performance 22
- Volunteer and Student Recognition 23

Sample Forms 24
- Program Development Plan Version I 24
- Program Development Plan Version II 25
- Class Schedule 26
- Volunteer Position Description 27
- Volunteer ESL Teacher or Tutor Agreement 28
- Volunteer and Student Intake and Placement Steps 29
- Student Intake Form 30
- Student Placement Card 32
- Student Needs Assessment 33
- Volunteer Evaluation 34
- Student Program Evaluation 36

Glossary 38

Resource Section 39

Expanding ESL, Civics, and Citizenship Education in Your Community

A Start-Up Guide

Many community, faith-based, and civic organizations and employers would like to help immigrants adjust to life in the United States and prepare for citizenship, but do not know where to begin. Fortunately, the experience and practices of existing English as a Second Language (ESL), civics, and citizenship programs for immigrants can help you get started. This guide offers suggestions and strategies gleaned from such programs, providing a framework you can adapt to suit your community's needs and circumstances.

This guide outlines a start-up process of gathering relevant information and resources to help you develop and sustain your program, recruit and train volunteers, and recruit students. It also includes basic recommendations and sample forms and materials to help you start your program.

This guide is not intended to be a curriculum. Curricula and teaching guidelines can be found through the U.S. Citizenship and Immigration Services (USCIS) resource entitled *U.S. Civics and Citizenship Online: Resource Center for Instructors*, located at http://www.uscis.gov/civicsonline, and through adult education publishers, local community colleges, and other Internet websites.

Using this guide to establish your program can help you offer a rewarding and important service to immigrants and your community.

TOPICS IN THIS GUIDE INCLUDE:

► Gathering Information and Basic Resources

► Program Design and Structure

► Staffing and Resources

► Marketing Your Program to Students

► Program Content and Instruction

► Program Development

A Start-Up Guide ► 1

Gathering Information and Basic Resources

Determining Community Needs

Part of starting a program is assessing the needs of your community and exploring the resources already available. If you are considering starting a program, it is likely you already know people in need of English language instruction at your place of worship, at your job, or in your neighborhood. However, there are ways to learn more about the needs of your community.

Gathering Information

You can contact community organizations and adult education programs currently providing services to immigrants to determine what ESL and civics/citizenship programming already exists in your community or nearby. Links such as http://www.welcometousa.gov can help you locate community organizations currently providing services in your area. This can help you learn about the level of unmet demand for English and civics/citizenship classes. For example, you may discover there is a local Mutual Assistance Association[1] that has a waiting list of people your program might help.

Meeting the Need

As you learn about existing programs in your area, you may find that your program could supplement services offered by other organizations. Partnerships with other organizations can enable you to offer additional support services to your students or to gather teaching materials and ideas from more experienced programs. If you find that there are few or no services of the kind you want to offer, your program can fill that gap.

---

[1] Mutual Assistance Associations, or MAAs, are community-based organizations managed primarily by and providing services to members of specific resettled refugee groups. These organizations can provide relevant information about specific ethnic groups, language groups, and cultures.

Program Design and Structure

Setting the Course for Your Program

Successful programs share several common elements, including creating a welcoming and participating environment for students and providing high-quality instruction. These programs help immigrants improve their English language ability so they can participate more fully in American life. Helping students learn to navigate America's many complex systems and to understand American culture will help them establish a new life in this country.

Assessing Your Resources
As you evaluate the services provided at your workplace or by community and faith-based organizations, resource centers, colleges, and libraries, keep in mind that existing programs may be able to assist with your start-up. You may discover you are surrounded by organizations with staff members who have teaching backgrounds, volunteer experience, or nonprofit coordination expertise. Consider a partnership as a way to supplement your program. Local programs can combine their services, such as meeting spaces, intake services, staff/interns/volunteers, transportation, childcare, and instruction, resulting in the ability to offer more concentrated services to the community.

Selecting the Target Audience
Consider the needs of all ages as you decide who will be your target group—adults, parents and children, seniors, refugees, etc.

Finding a Site
There are a variety of options for classroom space. You might consider such places as community centers, places of worship, libraries, local public schools, community college classrooms, and businesses (for example, a local company may offer a conference room). Accessibility for students and volunteers, including a safe and handicap accessible location, will increase participation. A site near public transportation or the availability of private transportation such as a van or carpool can help

A Start-Up Guide ▶ 3

facilitate attendance. Although not always feasible, finding a space designated specifically for your class is a good idea. This can foster a more personal and welcoming classroom setting. Students' ages and the types of activities you provide will determine the kinds of tables, chairs, and instructional equipment you need. A white board/chalk board, computers, DVD and CD players, and a secure place for teachers to store books, files, and teaching materials can enhance the learning environment.

Establishing a Program Framework and Mission[2]

Setting a clear program framework and objectives will provide structure and guidance for your program. Writing a mission statement for your program can help others understand its purpose. Identify how your program will be structured and

---

[2] Adapted from EL Civics "How-To" Manual, Bronx Community College of the City University of New York, U.S. Department of Education. 2003.

supported by staff members. Each program is unique, but some elements common to most programs offering ESL and civics/citizenship instruction include:

- Providing English language instruction, including a civics and history component, to adult immigrants and refugees.

- Providing information to help immigrant families navigate American systems (such as schools, healthcare, government agencies, etc.).

- Helping eligible permanent residents prepare for U.S. citizenship.

Once you establish the framework for your program, you can outline specific plans and objectives for reaching those goals. Some sample objectives may include:

- We will name a program director and develop a staffing structure/plan.

- We will form a program planning committee by [date].

- We will create a program development plan by [date]. (This document will evolve over time.) You can tailor the sample program development plans on pages 24 and 25 to meet your program needs.

- We will approach two partner agencies to collaborate with us by [date].
- We will secure program resources (books, reference materials, etc.).
- We will recruit 15 volunteers by [date].
- We will train 10 volunteers by [date].
- We will recruit 30 students by [date].
- We will enroll 15 students by [date].
- We will start classes on [date].

Program Structure and Instruction

The instruction schedule you choose can vary, including morning, afternoon, or evening classes, weekend classes, and classes held several days in a row or daily each week. It is important to take into account work schedules, family obligations, childcare, and transportation needs as you develop a class schedule. You can tailor the sample class schedule on page 26 to meet your program needs.

Class Size

You may choose to offer instruction in a variety of formats, including one-on-one tutoring, small groups, or large classes. The number of teachers, volunteers, and students; students' English ability levels; and available space are factors to consider in deciding what type of instruction to offer. One-on-one tutoring matches one volunteer with one student. Small groups usually have two to six students. Large classes can have 20 or more students.

Instructional Approach

The number of teachers that your program needs will depend on the number of students, type of class, and teaching style you believe will best meet the needs of the students. One option, team teaching, usually involves two teachers providing instruction to a large class. This structure allows teachers to break a large class into smaller groups based on ability level. In some team teaching environments, teachers alternate teaching days with the same class. This structure also enables teachers to support one another in planning and teaching and reduces the need for substitute teachers.

Another approach may involve one-on-one tutoring with a teacher or volunteer.

Enrollment Options

You may find that classes that have a fee associated with them have a better retention rate. However, class fees generally do not sustain a program, but rather encourage students to commit to the class/program. Open-entry/open-exit programs allow students to enroll in class at any point during the year and withdraw when they have met their individual learning goals. One advantage of this structure is that students need not wait until the next term to begin classes. This helps avoid problems associated with delaying enrollment, such as students' loss of interest and motivation.

Setting enrollment cycles or terms is an alternative that can provide predictability and continuity for both students and teachers. You may want to provide four- to seven-week cycles, during which all students begin and end instruction at the same time. Some programs operate on a semester system. You can decide how many weeks of classes to hold in a session based on how many units you will be teaching. While there are a variety of program designs, in federally funded adult ESL programs, 50 hours of instruction is typically used as the benchmark in determining if students have improved their skills.

Staffing and Resources

Finding and Supporting Your Volunteers

Volunteer Positions

Volunteers can participate in many ways. Let prospective volunteers know what type of help you are seeking and match their interests with your program needs. You may need:

- Teachers
- Administrative personnel
- Program coordinator
- One-on-one tutors
- Classroom tutors
- Conversation group leaders
- Conversation partners
- Workshop leaders or trainers
- Curriculum developers
- Mentors/coaches
- Childcare providers

Volunteer Job Descriptions

Once you have an idea of the kinds of positions necessary for your program, you can develop volunteer job descriptions stating the qualifications and time commitments for tutors and other volunteer positions. It will help to specify the qualifications you are looking for in your program volunteers, such as fluency in English, writing skills, a high school diploma or GED, college degree, etc. You may have different requirements for different positions. For example, a good tutor or teacher does not necessarily need advanced education. Volunteer tutoring usually requires time to prepare lessons in addition to classroom teaching hours, so when volunteers are deciding how much time they can devote, they need to understand the schedule requirements. You can tailor the sample volunteer position description on page 27 to meet your program needs. A signed agreement or contract outlining your expectations of volunteers and the work they will perform can help clarify the time and effort involved. Limiting the length of the commitment period may help encourage a volunteer to sign up initially. You can tailor the sample agreement on page 28 to meet your program needs.

Volunteer Tutor Recruitment

Once you determine the volunteers and skills your program needs to operate, you can recruit volunteers with those skills. You may already know people who are interested in volunteering to teach English to adult immigrants and their families or helping meet other program needs. If you have not yet identified volunteers, there are many ways to begin recruiting efforts.

A Start-Up Guide ▶ 7

Nonprofit program participants may be willing to give back to the community. Check with local programs for referrals. Word-of-mouth referrals of your program can help raise awareness, as can having your program director or coordinator speak at community events. You can post flyers on community bulletin boards or ask local businesses to post them in their buildings. You may also consider placing notices in local English language and non-English language newspapers to attract both native English speakers and multilingual individuals who would like to help people who speak the same language.

You may want to post messages on online bulletin boards to solicit volunteer help. See if you can advertise your volunteer tutoring opportunities in the newsletters produced by places of worship or other organizations. Additionally, you may want to consider hosting an outreach table if your community holds volunteer activity fairs.

Consider contacting local undergraduate and graduate programs in TESOL (Teachers of English to Speakers of Other Languages), as these and other education programs often have students who are seeking hands-on teaching experience. These students may want to volunteer or serve as teaching interns. Retired professionals can also serve as excellent volunteers because they often have a variety of skills and more flexible schedules.

Across the country, many literacy and adult education coalitions offer technical assistance and support to volunteer programs. Literacy USA is a nonprofit membership organization that works closely with these coalitions. Another nonprofit membership organization, ProLiteracy Worldwide, supports literacy programs nationwide and accredits volunteer literacy programs. Both organizations maintain databases and contacts with adult education providers across the United States, and can be a source of volunteers and other resources.

If you notify both local and national volunteer clearinghouses that you are seeking tutors or teachers, these organizations may be able to post a notice in their online and print publications. National literacy directories, such as America's Literacy Directory, provide contact information for organizations throughout the country. America's Literacy Directory has partnered with the National Institute for Literacy, the U.S. Department of Education, the U.S. Department of Labor, and Verizon. Visit http://www.literacydirectory.org for more information.

In addition, you can list your opportunities at http://www.serve.gov. This website promotes volunteer service in America by partnering with national service programs and helping to connect individuals with volunteer opportunities. This is one of the largest volunteer service databases in the country and would serve as an excellent starting point for posting your volunteer opportunities.

Introducing the Program to Volunteers

You may wish to create a simple brochure or document outlining the purpose, objectives, and organizational structure of your program. This material will be helpful not only in volunteer recruitment, but also in your overall outreach efforts.

Volunteer Screening and Selection

Interviewing volunteers will help build a high-quality program. Volunteer tutors should be willing to learn and develop teaching skills and should be flexible in trying new strategies to address student needs and learning styles. Remember, you are not required to accept every potential volunteer into your program.

Potential volunteers can come from a variety of backgrounds. Volunteers do not need to speak languages other than English to teach in your program, but it may be helpful if they do. Such volunteers will be able to communicate with students with limited English comprehension and may understand the challenges of learning a new language. Volunteers are also not required to have a background in teaching. This experience would be beneficial, especially for teacher training opportunities, but should not be an absolute requirement.

Volunteer Orientation

Once your recruitment efforts spark interest in your program, you can hold an information session for prospective volunteers. You can discuss the mission of your program, expectations for volunteers, how they will be evaluated, time commitments, policies and procedures, and the types of support they will receive. Orientations can be conducted individually or in group sessions.

Background information describing the program and introducing prospective volunteers to the staff and students is helpful in enabling prospective volunteers to decide if they want to make a commitment to your program. Identifying the roles of staff members and structure of your program will help volunteers have a better understanding of how your program works.

Volunteer Support and Tutor Training

All volunteers, including those with prior teaching experience, need support so they can develop as instructors and best contribute to your program. Community partnerships can be very helpful at this point. Experienced groups that have designed and conducted volunteer training programs may be helpful to your ESL and civics/citizenship program.

Local Resources

If there is a literacy coalition near you, you can contact the organization and ask what type of training resources it offers to both volunteer and professional staff. Some local coalitions not only support existing programs with training and resources, but also provide tools and technical support to fledgling volunteer programs. They may offer online resources on instructional methods as well.

National Resources

USCIS has developed a variety of training and technical resources to support volunteers and adult educators. These include:

- EL/Civics Online: A series of free online training modules for instructors and volunteers who wish to incorporate EL/civics content into their adult ESL programs: http://www.elcivicsonline.org/.
- *U.S. Civics and Citizenship Online: Resource Center for Instructors:* A web-based tool offering teachers and volunteers a single source for locating resources to incorporate civics and citizenship into ESL instruction: http://www.uscis.gov/civicsonline.
- Training Workshops: Free professional development opportunities, convened by USCIS, to help refine skills and prepare volunteers and adult educators for teaching U.S. history, civics, and the naturalization process to immigrant students. Visit http://www.uscis.gov/teachertraining for more information.

Other organizations providing training and professional development resources for volunteers and adult educators include:

- Thinkfinity Literacy Network: http://www.thinkfinity.org/
- Outreach and Technical Assistance Network: http://www.otan.dni.us/
- Center for Adult English Language Acquisition: http://www.cal.org/caela/
- ProLiteracy Worldwide: http://www.proliteracy.org/

See the sample volunteer and student intake and placement steps on page 29 as a guideline for initiating volunteers.

Marketing Your Program to Students

Getting Students Involved

Student Recruitment

There are several ways to help advertise your program to prospective students. It is important to remember that recruitment is an ongoing process. Give your program sufficient time to recruit enough students to meet your program's goals.

Flyers

You can design a flyer with program information and post it in the neighborhood near the location where you plan to hold classes (in both English and other common languages spoken in your community). A free option is using billboards or displays in areas with heavy foot-traffic, such as on public transportation or at public transportation stops. Place flyers in stores frequented by immigrants, or ask businesses that cater to non-English-speaking customers if they would place your flyers in their shopping bags or on a bulletin board. Consider contacting local schools to see if it is possible to post flyers in their offices. Other places to consider are places of worship and community organizations. Also, local businesses may be willing to place notices in paycheck envelopes or other employee correspondence to inform employees and their family members of your program.

Presentations

Ask local schools if you can give a presentation at open houses to inform parents about your program. You can contact places of worship and ask if it would be possible to give a presentation or place an announcement in the newsletter or weekly announcements. Many community organizations hold fairs and bazaars during which representatives from community groups speak and disseminate information about the services they offer. You can find out when these events are scheduled and take the opportunity to introduce your program.

Media

Many communities have ethnic newspapers targeted at specific populations. You may be able to place translated advertisements in these newspapers or list your program's information in the "Classifieds" section. Local radio stations may be willing to place short public service announcements (PSAs) about your program. If possible, translate each advertisement or PSA into the language commonly spoken in the local community.

Referrals

Notify other service organizations in the community, such as social service offices, food banks, or housing authorities, about your classes so that the staff there can refer their clients to your program.

Online

Consider listing your program on the America's Literacy Directory database at http://www.literacydirectory.org. This national database lists literacy programs available in all 50 states and the U.S. territories. You can also post your program information on electronic bulletin boards and community websites. While many prospective learners may not be searching the Internet, their friends and relatives may share what they learn about your program.

Word of Mouth

A powerful recruitment tool is a recommendation by a satisfied student. You can encourage current and former students to help in your recruitment efforts. Also, encourage your volunteers to mention the program to their colleagues, friends, and neighbors in the community.

Student Registration and Orientation

Potential students may be unfamiliar with the types of classes offered, the structure of the organization, or the various teaching methods used in your program. Below are several suggestions to help explain the enrollment process.

Intake and Registration

It can help if program staff meet one-on-one with prospective students to fill out intake paperwork and obtain relevant contact and background information. You can include personal, educational, and employment goals, learning interests, special needs, and schedule availability. You can find out if students are working and have families, where they are from, how many languages they know, or how many years of formal schooling they have completed. Fees may also be collected during the intake and registration process.

The sample intake forms on pages 30 and 31 can be tailored to meet your program needs.

Students who cannot communicate in English may come to register for classes with a friend or family member who speaks English and can interpret. Giving students appropriate program information in writing will let them know when to return for classes or assessment testing. If possible, you can provide intake and assessment materials for students in their native language. Interpreter and translation services can be a benefit of a community partnership. You can tailor the sample placement card on page 32 to meet your program needs. See the sample volunteer and student intake and placement process flow chart on page 29 as a guideline for enrolling students.

Orientation
After one-on-one meetings with prospective students, it is helpful to provide a group orientation to introduce students to the various classes, teachers, and support services available at your program.

Program Content and Instruction

Determining Student Educational Needs: What and How to Teach

Needs Assessment

You can learn about your students' interests and needs by providing a list of topic areas for them to review and select so that you can ascertain what areas they would like to study. You can offer this in picture or text form. You can tailor the sample needs assessment form on page 33 to meet your program needs.

Informal and Formal Assessment[3]
There are a variety of methods for measuring your students' current skill levels and development, and you should select those that suit

---
[3]Forlizzi, Lori. Pennsylvania Department of Education. http://www.pde.state.pa.us/able.

your program's needs. Informal and formal assessments help identify the areas in which students need help and the subjects they want to study. These assessments can aid you in making decisions about curriculum and instruction and assist students in setting short- and long-term learning goals. Assessments can be given at the beginning, middle, and end of a program.

Informal assessments provide flexible ways to determine student needs and abilities. Such assessments can be found in the front of textbooks and used to check students' knowledge before they start their studies. You can also develop your own informal assessments to measure students' subject matter knowledge and their English language comprehension, listening, and speaking abilities. Try asking written questions about the content you will be teaching, questioning students orally, or requiring them to perform a certain task.

Formal, or standardized, assessments are those administered with standard and consistent conditions and procedures such as timing, instructions, scoring, and interpretation. Some formal assessments commonly used by adult ESL programs are the Basic English Skills Test (BEST), produced by the Center for Applied Linguistics (CAL), and the Comprehensive Adult Student Assessment Systems (CASAS), which has been approved and validated by the U.S. Department of Education and the U.S. Department of Labor. Although initially your program may not want to invest in these commercially produced standardized tests, you may want to consider using them in the future if you plan to expand your program and seek funding that requires such performance reporting.

A Start-Up Guide ▶ 15

Topics Often Included in ESL/Civics Instruction

Sample topics include:
- U.S. history and government
- Rights and responsibilities of legal permanent residents and U.S. citizens
- Information on the naturalization process
- Housing
- Childcare
- School systems
- Financial systems
- Community and home safety
- Emergencies
- Health
- Transportation

Teaching Resources

As mentioned in the National Resources section on pages 10-11, many resources are readily available for use in adult ESL and civics/citizenship programs. Many of these materials may be used free of charge. You may also want to seek out established adult education centers in your area, such as community colleges, that have already developed curricula and lesson plans that may be useful in your program. Established programs may offer recommendations for materials from commercial publishers specializing in adult education books and other materials for purchase.

Curricula and Resources

The Internet is a valuable source for identifying curricula and developing instructional plans and educational resources. Some useful resources from USCIS are listed below.

Resources from U.S. Citizenship and Immigration Services

Located at http://www.uscis.gov, the USCIS website offers a variety of free teaching resources for adult educators. Some of these materials include *Welcome to the United States: A Guide for New Immigrants*, available in a variety of foreign languages, Civics Flash Cards, and *Learn About the United States: Quick Civics Lessons*. Each of these publications can be used as a stand-alone resource for individual study or as a teaching tool in a classroom setting.

In addition, USCIS offers the Civics and Citizenship Multimedia Presentation, a 2-disc set which includes the short film *A Promise of Freedom: An Introduction to U.S. History and Civics for Immigrants* and the Flash® presentation *Becoming a U.S. Citizen: An Overview of the Naturalization Process.*

Instruction

- U.S. Department of State's Bureau of International Information Programs website, located at http://www.america.gov, includes a variety of materials for those seeking to learn more about American society, political processes, and U.S. history and government.

- Community Partnerships for Adult Learning, located at http://www.c-pal.net, is a website supported by the U.S. Department of Education containing resources designed to improve the accessibility and quality of adult education. The website provides links to how-to manuals, lesson plans, curricula, research, and standards.

Content Standards

Many states have content standards outlining specific skills, behaviors, and task performance adults should demonstrate to be successful in school, work, and the community. You can view these on the U.S. Department of Education's Adult Education Content Standards Warehouse website at http://www.adultedcontentstandards.ed.gov/. These materials offer samples of the types of topics and skills taught in ESL programs around the country.

Teaching Techniques

There are many methods for teaching and tutoring in ESL, civics, and citizenship. Do not be afraid to try a variety of approaches to see what works best for your program, your volunteers, and your students.

ProLiteracy Worldwide outlines several different methods to help students learn. Students should **hear** about the topic, **see** things about the topic, **ask** questions about the topic,

A Start-Up Guide ▶ 17

discuss the topic, and *do* something related to the topic. Other ideas from ProLiteracy Worldwide include[4]:

- Providing opportunities for students to identify what they want to learn.
- Working with students to set realistic short-term goals that will help them progress toward their long-term goals.
- Planning multisensory activities, such as listening to songs or practicing related vocabulary when tasting foods or going to the grocery store, library, or museum. Engaging in activities while learning related vocabulary and communication skills can help all students, especially learners unaccustomed to working with textbooks.
- Allowing students to work in pairs or groups.
- Talking about the purpose of different learning activities before you do them.
- Checking student comprehension and comfort with new material.
- Connecting students' daily lives to your instruction by using real-life materials, such as a workplace manual, an apartment lease, or a medical brochure.
- Asking students regularly about their satisfaction with their learning.
- Involving students in the development of lesson plans.
- Helping students see the progress they are making.
- Offering multiple opportunities for students to practice.
- Asking questions that encourage students to share their ideas and solve problems.
- Providing feedback throughout instruction.

---

[4] *Promising Practices, Increasing Intensity of Instruction in Volunteer-Based Literacy Programs.* Developed by ProLiteracy America with funding from UPS. 2007.

Learning Styles

Learning styles and learning preferences vary among individuals. Some learning styles include visual, auditory, tactile, and kinesthetic. **Visual** learners learn best through seeing. This includes written information, diagrams, the face and gestures of the speaker, items written on the board, charts, and video. **Auditory** learners learn through hearing. They understand best when they can hear lectures, participate in conversations, read aloud, or listen to recordings. **Tactile** learners learn through touch. They learn best when they move around and handle and manipulate objects. **Kinesthetic** learners learn by doing. They need hands-on activities to understand how something works or what it means. Teaching with these learning styles in mind will help you meet the various needs of your students.

Creating a Supportive Learning Environment

Teachers, tutors, and students will feel comfortable in an environment that encourages participation. Playing games and incorporating music and singing are low-stress ways to use language and have fun. Encourage students to share their ideas in class and with program administrators. You can foster student involvement by creating a student leadership council or asking students to become tutors as they progress in their language abilities. Invite students to provide feedback on the program.

While instruction will address topics and problem-solving skills that can assist students in their daily lives, tutors should not be expected to solve their students' problems. When students and families face challenges that your volunteers are unable to address, you can refer the students to community partners and social service organizations for assistance. Students also may have issues with their immigration cases. These students should be referred to an organization with Board of Immigration Appeals (BIA) accredited staff or to a licensed immigration attorney. For a list of organizations, see http://www.usdoj.gov/eoir/statspub/accreditedreproster.pdf. Your staff and volunteers should not try to counsel students on their own.

Program Development

How to Strengthen Your Program

Start-Up Costs and Sustainability

There are a variety of potential costs involved in developing and sustaining your program. Start-up costs include everything from recruiting students to purchasing furniture and teaching supplies. Sustained costs could include paying rent and utilities, purchasing equipment and supplies, and recruitment and retention efforts for both students and teachers.

Outreach

Outreach to students and volunteers can involve costs for flyers, brochures, or newsletters, whether produced in-house or by a professional printer. Professional printing can be expensive, but depending on the number of materials you want to produce, it may be a helpful option. You may also want to consider buying an advertisement in community magazines and newspapers, which could prove worthwhile for your program.

Training Volunteers

If you are unable to find an organization or individual who can provide training for your volunteer tutors, you will need to develop your own training materials and activities. This will entail writing and printing a manual, providing supplies for the trainees, locating a place for the training, and finding someone to conduct the training.

Classroom Space

If you do not have your own classroom space, you may need to pay a small fee to use space owned or leased by another organization, or ask another organization to donate space.

Teaching Materials

Many free teaching resources are available through USCIS and other entities. However, you may also want to purchase adult or family literacy workbooks from publishers specializing in adult education and family literacy.

Refreshments
Consider offering refreshments before class or during class breaks, since many students may come to your class directly from work. You may also want to provide refreshments at meetings and training sessions for volunteers.

Funding and Coordination
Although there are a variety of costs associated with providing ESL and civics/citizenship classes to adult students, there are many creative ways to finance your program. Programs that do not receive federal, state, or private funding can generate financial support through fundraising or other activities. These programs often develop relationships with local businesses that will sponsor activities by providing advertising or donating supplies. Businesses may go as far as to house your program if they feel their employees can directly benefit from it.

Starting and coordinating a volunteer program can take a lot of time and resources, so you may want to consider offering a small stipend to a volunteer who can lead these efforts. You may also want to establish partnerships with programs that offer complementary services or in-house expertise.

Fundraising
There are a variety of fundraising options you can use to help fund your ESL and civics/citizenship program. Proceeds from an event such as a fair, talent show, concert, auction, yard sale, bake sale, or car wash could be used to support your program. You may also want to ask a local business to sponsor your program by supplying funds for materials, or donating classroom space or other services. If you have experience fundraising for other purposes, you can apply it to your ESL and civics/citizenship program.

Grants
A variety of grant programs and funding opportunities exist. You can learn about federal government grant opportunities and if you are eligible to apply from http://www.grants.gov. The National Institute for Literacy's website, located at http://www.nifl.gov, features a Grants and Funding Database listing funding opportunities. Other organizations such as the Foundation Center and the Grantsmanship Center provide resources and training on fundraising, proposal writing, and program planning. Books on grant writing and fundraising are available at local libraries and bookstores.

Evaluating Program Performance

You will want to evaluate your program regularly. This will help you know if you are serving your students and volunteers effectively and help you know what changes you need to make. You should build in program flexibility so you can more easily adjust to the levels and needs of your students.

Measuring Program Performance

Review the objectives you set when designing the program and see how much progress you have accomplished. It is important to examine other performance indicators, such as volunteer and student attendance and overall retention. For example, dropout rates exist in both populations because adults have many demands on their time. Volunteers may get other jobs, and students may move or change shifts at work. However, sometimes students and volunteers leave because they are unsatisfied with the quality of the program, or volunteers leave because they do not feel prepared or supported by the program's leadership. Therefore, it is useful to examine retention rates and other measures of program performance in order to make any necessary adjustments.

Assessing Student Performance

You can use formal and informal assessments to measure student progress (see page 15). Conducting pre-tests and post-tests will show you if students are improving their skills. You can create your own tests and administer them at both the beginning and end of a unit to determine what the students have learned. Maintaining a folder of written work or audio- or videotapes of students speaking is a great way to capture their individual progress over time.

Volunteer Input

Encourage volunteers to provide feedback on the program. You could hold volunteer meetings, establish a volunteer council, or provide a suggestion box. You can tailor the sample volunteer evaluation on pages 34-35 to meet your program needs.

Student Input

Provide an anonymous method for students to evaluate volunteers, and give feedback about what they consider effective instruction.

This will enable tutors to understand student perceptions and consider student suggestions for improvement. You can tailor the sample student program evaluation on pages 36-37 to meet your program needs.

Follow-up
To assess the long-term impact of your program, try to maintain contact with students after they leave the program. Follow-up could be done through phone calls, e-mail contact, alumni events, or offering advanced English workshops or classes that may renew former students' interest in your program. Successful graduates can help motivate current and prospective students and offer a sense of satisfaction to the teachers who contributed to their success.

Volunteer and Student Recognition

It is important to thank your volunteers and to recognize your students' achievements. Consider some simple, tangible offerings to acknowledge their work, such as a certificate, pen, tote bag, or t-shirt, which local business may be willing to donate. You might present these at a social gathering or awards ceremony. Another effective way to recognize student performance is to ask current or former students to serve as program volunteers. Many former students would consider this invitation a great honor.

Partnerships
Keep in mind that partnerships and collaboration with other service providers can supply important complementary services to your program, such as childcare, housing assistance, case management, and employment training.

Good Luck!

Using these basic guidelines for starting an ESL and civics/citizenship program will put you well on your way to a successful experience for both your volunteers and your students. Enjoy the wonderful relationships you develop and the satisfaction of helping improve the lives and opportunities of those in your community.

SAMPLE
PROGRAM DEVELOPMENT PLAN
Version I

Task: Recruit "x" number of additional planning committee members
Products or results of task performed: Four-person volunteer planning committee
Who is responsible: Core volunteer person/group
Target Completion Date: Oct. 1, 20XX
Actual Completion Date: _____

Task: Secure location
Products or results of task performed: Classroom space
Who is responsible: Volunteer planning committee
Target Completion Date: Dec. 1, 20XX
Actual Completion Date: _____

Task: Outline class or program goals
Products or results of task performed: Written goals
Who is responsible: Volunteer planning committee
Target Completion Date: Jan. 15, 20XX
Actual Completion Date: _____

Task: Outline class or program objectives
Products or results of task performed: Written objectives
Who is responsible: Volunteer planning committee
Target Completion Date: Jan. 15, 20XX
Actual Completion Date: _____

Task: Name a program director
Products or results of task performed:
Who is responsible:
Target Completion Date:
Actual Completion Date: _____

Task:
Products or results of task performed:
Who is responsible:
Target Completion Date:
Actual Completion Date: _____

Task:
Products or results of task performed:
Who is responsible:
Target Completion Date:
Actual Completion Date: _____

SAMPLE
PROGRAM DEVELOPMENT PLAN
Version II

Task	Products or results of task performed	Who is responsible	Target Completion Date	Actual Completion Date
Recruit "x" number of additional planning committee members	Four-person volunteer planning committee	Core volunteer person/group	Oct. 1, 20XX	
Secure class location	Classroom space	Volunteer planning committee	Dec. 1, 20XX	
Outline class or program goals	Written goals	Volunteer planning committee	Jan. 15, 20XX	
Outline class or program objectives	Written objectives	Volunteer planning committee	Jan. 15, 20XX	
Develop volunteer recruitment strategy	A specific plan for recruiting volunteer tutors	Volunteer planning committee	Jan. 15, 20XX	
Implement volunteer recruitment strategy	3 flyer designs, 2 newspaper ads, 1 PSA, 1 announcement in a faith-based weekly bulletin or newsletter	Volunteer planning committee	Jan. 15 – Mar. 15, 20XX	
Develop volunteer orientation	Agenda, handouts, etc.	Volunteer planning committee	Feb./Mar. 20XX	
Hold orientation	Orient 15 volunteers	Volunteer planning committee	Mar. 20, 20XX	
Send volunteers to training	10 trained volunteers	Lead volunteer	Apr. 20, 20XX	
Design student recruitment campaign	3 flyer designs, 2 newspaper ads, 1 PSA, 1 announcement in a faith-based weekly bulletin or newsletter	Volunteer planning committee	Mar. – May, 20XX	

SAMPLE
CLASS SCHEDULE

Three types of classes are held at this program:
1. ESL, Beginning level
2. ESL & Citizenship/Civics Intermediate level
3. ESL & Citzenship/Civics, Family Literacy
   (for parents/caregivers and their children ages birth–7 years)

	Monday	Tuesday	Wednesday	Thursday	Friday	Saturday
Morning	ESL Beginners 9:00–11:00	ESL Beginners 9:00–11:00	ESL Beginners 9:00–11:00	ESL Beginners 9:00–11:00	Tutor Meetings	ESL Beginners 9:00–12:00
Afternoon						ESL & Citizenship/ Civics Family Literacy 1:00–3:00
Evening		ESL & Citizenship/ Civics Intermediate 6:30–8:30	ESL & Citizenship/ Civics Intermediate 6:30–8:30	ESL & Citizenship/ Civics Intermediate 6:30–8:30		

SAMPLE
VOLUNTEER POSITION DESCRIPTION

Position Title: ESL Tutor

Qualifications: Ability to speak, read, and write English; respectful of cultural differences; flexible; desire to develop teaching skills.

Training: Participate in nine-hour training workshop and minimum of four hours of follow-up training throughout service.

Time Commitment: Minimum of six months; expect at least two hours in-class and one hour of preparation per week.

Responsibilities:

- Assist each student in setting goals.
- Prepare lesson for each class meeting.
- Arrive for teaching at least 15 minutes before start of class.
- Implement teaching techniques provided in tutor training and tutor manual.
- Participate in performance evaluation, including lesson reviews and teaching observations by coordinator.
- Provide attendance roster, lesson plan outlines, and progress reports to coordinator each month.
- Notify coordinator in advance if you are unable to teach a session.
- Be willing to consider participating in additional program activities and fundraisers.

Benefits:

- Opportunity to make an important contribution to your community and nation.
- Opportunity to learn new skills.
- Opportunity to meet people in your community and from around the world.

SAMPLE

VOLUNTEER ESL TEACHER OR TUTOR AGREEMENT

The duties of Volunteer ESL Tutors:

- I agree to tutor for a minimum of six months.
- I will attend nine hours of ESL tutor training before I begin tutoring.
- I will participate in four hours of additional training throughout the year.
- I will tutor for a minimum of two hours per week.
- I will spend at least one hour preparing for each class session.
- I will notify the lead volunteer if I must miss class, so that a substitute can be arranged.
- I understand that I may be asked to participate in fundraising efforts and other community activities.

Volunteer Tutor: _____

Signature: _____ Date: _____

Lead Volunteer: _____

Signature: _____ Date: _____

SAMPLE
VOLUNTEER AND STUDENT INTAKE AND PLACEMENT STEPS

Volunteers

Conduct volunteer outreach and recruitment:
Post flyers, place ads in print and online, make presentations, etc.

▼

Orient volunteers:
In a group setting, share the mission, expectations, time commitment, policies and procedures, etc.

▼

Screen volunteers:
Ask prospective volunteers to contact you following the orientation. Interview them and select those who meet your criteria.

▼

Train volunteers:
Provide training or send volunteers to a more established program to receive training.

▼

Match volunteers with students:
Assign volunteers to work with a student, a small group, or a class.

Students

Conduct student outreach and recruitment:
Post flyers, place ads in print and online, make presentations, etc.

↓

Orient and enroll students:
Based on staffing, hold drop-in enrollment or an orientation session to register many students at one time.

↓

Conduct intake with students:
Fill out intake paperwork and learn about their needs, English abilities, family and work obligations, previous education, etc.

↓

Place students:
Assign students to tutoring pairs, small groups, or classes based on English language level, schedule, and openings.

↓

Conduct further assessment:
Expand your understanding of students' listening, speaking, reading, and writing abilities by using informal or formal assessments.

SAMPLE
STUDENT INTAKE FORM
ESL/Civics/Citizenship Program

Date: _____ Staff Member: _____

Name: _____ Sex: __ male __ female

Address: _____

Phone: (h) _____ (c) _____ (w) _____

Date of Birth: _____/_____/_____

Family:
Marital Status: __ Married __ Single __ Divorced

Children: # _____ Ages: _____

Daycare: __ has children in daycare __ needs daycare for children __ N/A

Number of family members living in the home: _____

Student's country of birth: _____

Number of years living in the United States: _____

*Student is a __ citizen __ permanent resident __ refugee __ other

Education and Employment:

Has student taken ESL classes before? __ yes __ no

If yes, where? _____

When? _____

For how long? _____

What level did the student get to? _____

Languages student speaks: _____

Language spoken most at home: _____

Does student read and write in that language? _____

Highest level of school completed in native country: _____

Highest level of school completed in the United States: _____

Currently employed? _____

Place of employment and type of work:

_____

Student's class availability:

	Monday	Tuesday	Wednesday	Thursday	Friday	Saturday
Morning (9:00–12:00)						
Afternoon (1:00–4:00)						
Evening (5:00–8:30)						

Other notes:

---

* If students want to prepare for U.S. citizenship, refer them to a Board of Immigration Appeals (BIA) representative.

A Start-Up Guide ▶ 31

SAMPLE
STUDENT PLACEMENT CARD

ESL/Civics/Citizenship Program
Program Address
Program Phone Number

Student Name: _____

Date of Registration: _____

    Begin Class: <u>6/25/20XX</u> _____

    Tutor/Teacher: <u>Jane Smith</u> _____

    Location: <u>Jefferson Community Center</u> ___
           <u>123 Main Street</u> _____
           <u>Room B</u> _____

Class days and times:

Monday	Tuesday	Wednesday	Thursday	Friday
5:00 pm – 7:00 pm		5:00 pm – 7:00 pm		

Staff Member: _____

SAMPLE
STUDENT NEEDS ASSESSMENT
Excerpt 1

U.S. Government

	I know a lot	I know a little	I want to learn more	I don't want to learn more
How the federal government works				
Three branches of government				
State and local government				

Education

	I know a lot	I know a little	I want to learn more	I don't want to learn more
How to find childcare				
Elementary School				
High School				

SAMPLE
STUDENT NEEDS ASSESSMENT
Excerpt 2

I want to learn about:

__U.S. government   __Citizenship   __U.S. K-12 school system   __Housing   __Finding a job

A Start-Up Guide ▶ 33

SAMPLE
VOLUNTEER EVALUATION

*Please answer the following questions regarding your volunteer experience with _____
[program name]. We will use your feedback to improve the program for both volunteers and students.*

1 = strongly disagree   3 = unsure   5 = strongly agree

1. The training and information I received was relevant and useful   1 2 3 4 5
   in preparing me to volunteer in this program.

2. I have access to the materials and equipment I need to perform   1 2 3 4 5
   my volunteer service effectively.

3. The roles and responsibilities of my volunteer position are   1 2 3 4 5
   clearly defined.

4. There are staff members or other volunteers who support me   1 2 3 4 5
   in my efforts.

5. I feel that the program recognizes my volunteer efforts.   1 2 3 4 5

6. The space was conducive to tutoring (or other types of activities).   1 2 3 4 5

7. I enjoy volunteering with this program.   1 2 3 4 5

8. I would recommend this program to others seeking a   1 2 3 4 5
   volunteer experience.

9. What do you like about this program?

10. What recommendations do you have that will improve the experience
    for volunteers and students?

PLEASE CHECK ALL THAT APPLY:

11. What kind of preparation did the program provide to prepare you to volunteer?
    ___I attended a volunteer orientation session
    ___I was directed to community resources
    ___I attended in-service training
    ___I was mentored by an experienced volunteer
    ___I observed experienced volunteers
    ___Other _____

12. Do you have other skills you would like to use in your volunteer position?

13. In what areas would you like to receive more training or information?
    ___Assessment
    ___Lesson planning
    ___Instruction—general
    ___Instruction—specific topics _____
    ___Record keeping
    ___Classroom management
    ___Culture
    ___Other _____

Adapted from ProLiteracy Affiliates' Volunteer Satisfaction Surveys.

SAMPLE
STUDENT PROGRAM EVALUATION

Please fill out this form so that we can improve our classes. Please check all that apply and provide comments in the space next to your selection.

1. Things I like about the program.

                Check ✔   Please write why you like _____.

books and materials we used in class		
teaching by tutor or teacher		
topics we studied		
guest speakers		
students in program		
special events		
class location		
class day and time		
classroom		
amount of time in class		
OTHER:		

2. Things I do not like about the program.

       Check ✔ Please write why you do NOT like _____.

books and materials we used in class		
teaching by tutor or teacher		
topics we studied		
guest speakers		
students in program		
special events		
class location		
class day and time		
classroom		
amount of time in class		
OTHER:		

I know more about this topic because of this class:

  ___ U.S. history and government   ___ School systems

  ___ Rights and responsibilities of U.S. citizens ___ Financial systems

  ___ Rights and responsibilities of legal permanent residents ___ Community and home safety

  ___ Housing   ___ Emergencies

  ___ Health   ___ Transportation

  ___ Childcare

Other comments I have about this program:

Glossary

Assessment = Tools and processes used to evaluate the language level of students.

Board of Immigration Appeals (BIA) = The highest administrative body for interpreting and applying immigration laws. It is composed of 11 Board Members. *To learn more, see the U.S. Department of Justice website:* http://www.usdoj.gov/eoir/biainfo.htm.

Civics = Learning about the rights and responsibilities of citizenship, naturalization procedures, civic participation, and U.S. history and government; the skills and knowledge to become active and informed family and community members and workers.

Curriculum = Units of instruction aligned to provide students with specific knowledge. Units can consist of topics, chapters in a text, courses, etc.

ESL = English as a Second Language.

Evaluation = Measuring the performance of staff, students, and the program as a whole.

Indicators of Program Quality = Program characteristics or practices that show that the program is effectively meeting the needs of the students and the staff.

Intake = Procedures used by program staff to enroll students in the program.

Lesson Plan = Detailed plan of instruction developed by a teacher or tutor.

Standards = Descriptions of the skills, knowledge, or performance that should result from effective instruction. *To learn more, see the U.S. Department of Education's Adult Content Education Standards Warehouse website:* http://www.adultedcontentstandards.ed.gov/.

TESOL = Teachers of English to Speakers of Other Languages.

Resource Section

Introduction
http://www.uscis.gov/civicsonline

Gathering Information and Basic Resources
http://www.welcometousa.gov

Staffing and Resources
http://www.literacydirectory.org
http://www.serve.gov
http://www.elcivicsonline.org/
http://www.uscis.gov/civicsonline
http://www.uscis.gov/teachertraining
http://www.thinkfinity.org/
http://www.otan.dni.us/
http://www.cal.org/caela/
http://www.proliteracy.org/

Marketing Your Program to Students
http://www.literacydirectory.org

Program Content and Instruction
http://www.pde.state.pa.us/able
http://www.uscis.gov
http://www.america.gov
http://www.c-pal.net
http://www.adultedcontentstandards.ed.gov/
http://www.usdoj.gov/eoir/statspub/accreditedreproster.pdf

Program Development
http://www.grants.gov
http://www.nifl.gov

Glossary
http://www.usdoj.gov/eoir/biainfo.htm
http://www.adultedcontentstandards.ed.gov/